DinoZone

# PLANT-EATING DINOSAURS

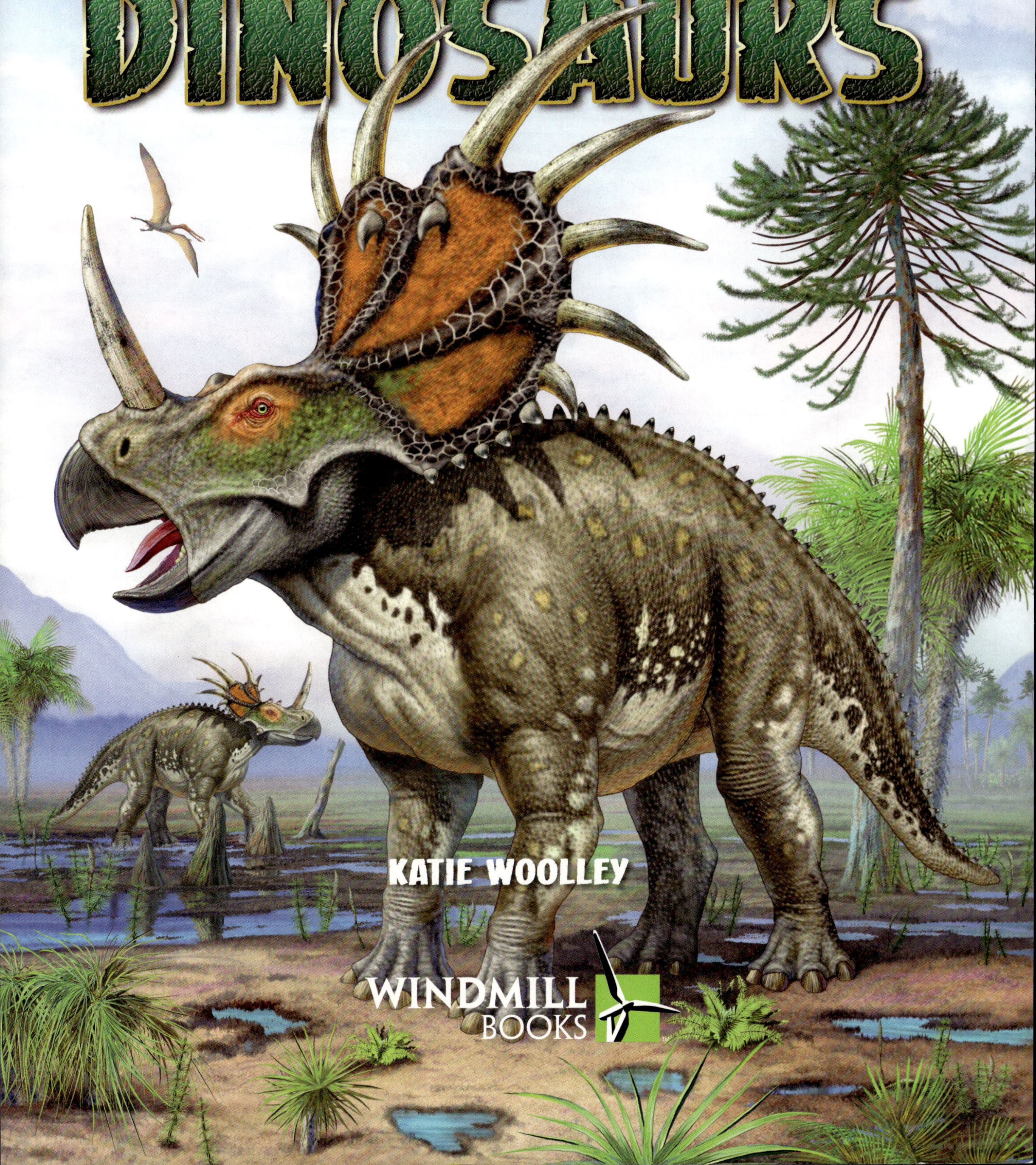

KATIE WOOLLEY

WINDMILL BOOKS

Published in 2017 by **Windmill Books**, an Imprint of Rosen Publishing
29 East 21st Street, New York, NY 10010



Author: Katie Woolley
Designers: Neal Cobourne and Emma Randall
Editors: Joe Harris and Anna Brett

Picture credits: Cover illustration: Rudolf Farkas

Interior illustrations: Arcturus Image Library (Stefano Azzalin: 8, 9, 14, 15, 18, 20, 23; Martin Bustamante: 4, 7t, 10, 11, 19t, 19b, 24, 25t, 25b, 26; Juan Calle: 12, 21; Colin Howard: 14c; Kunal Kundu: 17; Jerry Pyke: 16; Parwinder Singh: 22; Val Walerczuk: 13), Wikimedia Commons: 27t, and Shutterstock: 5, 6-7, 27b, 28-29.

Cataloging-in-Publication Data
Names: Woolley, Katie.
Title: Plant-eating dinosaurs / Katie Woolley.
Description: New York : Windmill Books, 2017. | Series: Dinozone | Includes index.
Identifiers: ISBN 9781499481709 (pbk.) | ISBN 9781499481716 (library bound) | ISBN 9781508192862 (6 pack)
Subjects: LCSH: Dinosaurs--Juvenile literature. | Herbivores, Fossil--Juvenile literature.
Classification: LCC QE861.5 W66 2017 | DDC 567.9--dc23

Manufactured in the United States of America
CPSIA Compliance Information: Batch #BW17PK: For Further Information contact Rosen Publishing, New York, New York at 1-800-237-9932

# CONTENTS

# Peaceful plant eaters

**About two thirds of dinosaurs were plant eaters, or herbivores. The biggest herbivores were enormous sauropods. Some sauropods ate enough plants every day to match the weight of a small car!**

*Brachiosaurus* (BRAH-kee-oh-SORE-us) was a sauropod living during the Jurassic period.

Most plant eaters had blunt teeth for stripping leaves from branches. Some, such as *Brachiosaurus*, walked on four legs. Others, such as *Plateosaurus* (PLAH-tee-oh-SORE-us), walked on two.

**Fast Facts**

Some dinosaurs swallowed rocks (gastroliths) to help break down the plants they'd eaten for lunch!

# A huge herbivore

**_Diplodocus_ (DIH-ploh-DOH-kus) was HUGE! Its tail was the longest of all the dinosaurs—as long as two tennis courts.**

*Diplodocus* had an enormous appetite. Its peg-shaped teeth could strip the tough leaves from conifers. It also ate leaves from other plants, such as gingkos, ferns, and horsetails.

In 1905, a cast of a *Diplodocus* skeleton was given to the Natural History Museum in London, UK. Its nickname is "Dippy!"

## Fast Facts

**When:** Late Jurassic period

**Food:** Leaves and soft plants

**Size:** 85 ft (26 m)

**Weight:** 27.5 tons (25,000 kg)

**How it moved:** Slowly, on four legs

**Found in:** United States

***Diplodocus*** **may have used its tail to whip predators!**

# Spiky protector

***Stegosaurus* (STEH-goh-SORE-us) was a large, slow-moving plant eater. It would have defended itself from predators with its powerful spiked tail.**

## Fast Facts

**When:** Late Jurassic period

**Food:** Leaves and plants

**Size:** 30 ft (9 m) long

**Weight:** 3.4 tons (3,100 kg )

**How it moved:** Slowly, on four legs

**Found in:** Worldwide

*Stegosaurus* had 17 bony plates on its back. They may have been used to keep the dinosaur cool, or to protect it from meat eaters. Or they may have been used for impressing possible mates.

***Stegosaurus'* tail spikes are called a "thagomizer."**

This dinosaur had a beak, like a bird. At the back of its mouth were small teeth called "cheek teeth" that it used to chew plant leaves.

*Stegosaurus* means **"roof lizard."**

# Three-horned threat

***Triceratops* had three horns on its face. It had a bony plate called a frill at the back of its skull. A predator would have to be pretty fearless to attack this dinosaur!**

*Triceratops* means **"three-horned face."**

This plant eater had a large head, about 10 feet (3 m) long. That's about a third of its 30-foot (9-m) length! *Triceratops* had a beak like a parrot's. Its cheek teeth helped it chew food.

***Triceratops'* frill may have made it look more impressive.**

## Fast Facts

**When:** Late Cretaceous period

**Food:** Leaves and plants

**Size:** 30 ft (9 m) long

You!

**Weight:** 6.1 tons (5,500 kg)

**How it moved:** On four legs

**Found in:** United States

*Triceratops* probably charged at its enemy, such as other *Triceratops* or predators like *T. rex*. It rushed with its head down and horns forward.

# Thick-headed lizard

***Pachycephalosaurus* (PAH-kee-seh-fah-low-SORE-us) had a thick skull, with a dome-shaped, bony lump on top. It used this tough part of its skull to ram other dinosaurs.**

This plant eater was probably a herd animal. Its thick skull might have been used to defend itself against predators, or in mating displays.

## Fast Facts

**When:** Late Cretaceous period

**Food:** Plants, fruit, and seeds

**Size:** 26 ft (8 m) long

**Weight:** 3.3 tons (3,000 kg)

**How it moved:** On two legs

**Found in:** Canada and United States

*Pachycephalosaurus* means

**"thick-headed lizard."**

**Pachycephalosaurus' skull was up to 10 inches (25 cm) thick!**

*Pachycephalosaurus* had bumpy knobs on its snout and around the dome on its head. However, its teeth were very small. It could not have eaten tough plants.

# Gentle giants

**Sauropods were the biggest animals that ever walked on land. *Mamenchisaurus'* (MAH-men-chee-SORE-us) neck alone was 42.6 feet (13 m) long. Its full height would have reached the top of a building with four floors!**

Sauropod means **"lizard-footed."**

Sauropods were the biggest dinosaurs. It would take a stack of three *T. rex* to reach the height of *Mamenchisaurus*!

An adult sauropod would have been too big to attack. Any predator that dared to get close enough would have been swiped by a sauropod's long tail.

Sauropods may have been big, but they had very small heads for their bodies. And they had even smaller brains! Luckily, these gentle giants didn't need to be clever.

# A spiny sauropod

***Amargasaurus* (ah-MAR-gah-SORE-us) was a migrating dinosaur that moved in herds searching for food. This plant eater may have eaten leaves whole, without even chewing its food before swallowing!**

A bizarre-looking dinosaur, *Amargasaurus* was smaller and had a shorter neck than most other sauropods. It may have looked for food on the ground, rather than up high.

## Fast Facts

**When:** Early Cretaceous period

**Food:** Tough plants

**Size:** 39 ft (12 m) long

**Weight:** 10 tons (9,000 kg)

**How it moved:** On four legs

**Found in:** Argentina, South America

The *Amargasaurus* cast in the Museum Victoria, Australia, is called "Margie."

*Amargasaurus* had two rows of spines along its back. These spines may have been joined by skin, so they looked like a sail. The "sail" may have been used for protection, in mating displays, or for keeping the dinosaur cool.

*Amargasaurus* means **"Amarga lizard."** La Amarga is a place in Argentina.

# Safety in numbers

**Some plant-eating dinosaurs lived in groups for protection, like zebra do today. They roamed in search of food. Some sauropods may have migrated great distances.**

Herding dinosaurs could warn each other of danger. *Parasaurolophus* (PAH-rah-sore-OH-loh-fus) was especially good at this. It could make a loud noise by pushing air into the hollow crest on top of its head.

*Parasaurolophus*

**Chasmosaurus** (KAZ-moh-SORE-us)

*Chasmosaurus* and *Centrosaurus* probably lived in large groups. Younger animals did not have horns. They would have been protected by older members of the herd.

**Centrosaurus** (SEN-troh-SORE-us)

# Spiky hands

***Iguanodon* (ig-WAH-no-don) was a plant-eating dinosaur that could move around on two or four legs. It had a toothless beak and cheek teeth, which it used to chew tough plants.**

This plant eater had a bendy little finger for grasping food, and sharp thumb claws for prying open tough fruits. The claws also protected it against predators.

## Fast Facts

**When:** Early Cretaceous period

**Food:** Plants

**Size:** 33 ft (10 m) long

**Weight:** 4.4 tons (4,000 kg)

**How it moved:** On two or four legs

**Found:** Worldwide

*Iguanadon* means **"iguana tooth."**

**Scientists used to think that *Iguanodon's* thumb claws were horns!**

*Iguanodon* lived during the Cretaceous period when Pangaea was breaking up into many continents. Fossils of this dinosaur have been found in North America, Europe, and Asia.

# A living tank

***Ankylosaurus* (AN-kuh-loh-SORE-us) was a big, heavy plant eater that moved slowly. Because of its large size, it needed to eat a lot of plants to stay alive!**

*Ankylosaurus* had short legs, so it walked fairly low to the ground. Its narrow beak and small teeth helped it strip leaves from low-lying plants.

***Ankylosaurus* could attack predators with the bony club at the end of its tail.**

## Fast Facts

**When:** Late Cretaceous period

**Food:** Plants

**Size:** 23 ft (7 m) long

**Weight:** 4.4 to 7.7 tons (4,000 to 7,000 kg)

**How it moved:** On four legs

**Found in:** Canada and United States

This dinosaur is possibly the most heavily protected dinosaur we know about. Its body was covered in thick bony plates, two rows of spikes, and large horns, and its tail was like a club. Its plates were probably made from keratin—the same stuff as your fingernails!

*Ankylosaurus* means **"stiff lizard."**

# Dinosaur defenders

**Scientists think that many plant eaters had tough, leathery skin. This was to protect them from the razor-sharp teeth of meat-eating dinosaurs. But many had other weapons they could use in an attack.**

Size was a big help! Only ferocious predators or pack hunters would try to kill a mighty sauropod, such as *Titanosaurus* (TIE-tan-oh-SORE-us). Others, such as *Tuojiangosaurus* (too-YANG-oh-sore-us) and *Styracosaurus* (sty-RAH-koh-SORE-us), protected themselves with horns, bony plates, and spikes.

*Styracosaurus*

Camouflage markings may have helped plant-eating dinosaurs blend into their surroundings. This way, hungry predators might not see them.

# Mother *Maiasaura*

**A fantastic fossil find in North America revealed a *Maiasaura* (my-ah-SORE-ah) nesting site. *Maiasaura* mothers laid their eggs in a circle and covered them with earth and leaves to keep them safe and warm.**

*Maiasaura* lived in herds to protect themselves from predators like *Troodon*. This is also why females laid their eggs together, so there was more than one adult to keep watch over the nests and young.

*Maiasaura* eggs were oval and around 6 inches (15 cm) long.

*Maiasaura* laid up to 30 eggs at a time in one nest. Once the eggs hatched the young were at risk of attack and they had to quickly learn how to fend for themselves.

## Fast Facts

**When:** Late Cretaceous period

**Food:** Leaves and plants

**Size:** 29.5 ft (9 m) long

**Weight:** 2.7 tons (2,500 kg )

**How it moved:** On two or four legs

**Found in:** United States

*Maiasaura* means **"good mother reptile."**

# Fossils around the world

**Plant-eating dinosaurs lived all over the world. We know this because of where their fossils have been found. Can you see a plant eater that would have existed near you?**

# Glossary

**appetite** A desire to eat food.

**camouflage** The appearance of an animal, which helps it to blend in with its surroundings.

**charge** To move forward quickly as an attack.

**continent** A very large area of land, mostly or completely surrounded by water. Modern Earth has seven continents.

**Cretaceous period** A period in Earth's history, between 144 and 65 million years ago.

**fearless** Not having any fear.

**ferocious** Fierce, violent, or aggressive.

**fossil** The remains or imprint of an animal or plant, preserved for millions of years, now turned to stone.

**gastrolith** A rock swallowed by a dinosaur to help break down tough plant material in its stomach.

**grasp** Grab and hold strongly.

**herd** A group of animals living together.

**Jurassic period** A time in Earth's history, between 206 and 144 million years ago.

**mate** The partner of an animal.

**migrate** To move from one place to another to find more food or better conditions.

**nest** A place chosen or made by an animal in which to lay its eggs.

**oval** A shape like a stretched circle.

**Pangaea** One vast area of land on Earth that existed before it broke up into separate continents.

**predator** An animal that eats other animals.

**ram** Crash violently against something else.

**roam** Move about a large area of land.

**sauropods** Large, plant-eating dinosaurs with long necks and tails.

**skeleton** A frame made up of all the bones in an animal's body.

**Triassic period** A period in Earth's history, between 248 and 206 million years ago.

**weapon** Something used to cause harm or damage.

**whip** To move something long and flexible quickly, in order to cause pain or damage.

# Further information

## Further reading

*The Complete Book of Dinosaurs* by Dougal Dixon (Southwater, 2012)

*Dinosaur Encyclopedia* by Caroline Bingham (DK Children's, 2009)

*Dinosaurs* by Stephanie Turnbull (Usborne, 2006)

*Jurassic Record Breakers* by Darren Naish (Carlton Kids, 2015)

*National Geographic Little Kids Big Book of Dinosaurs* by Catherine D. Hughes (National Geographic Children's Books, 2011)

*Planet Dinosaur* by editors of the BBC (BBC Books, 2011)

## Websites

For web resources related to the subject of this book, go to: **www.windmillbooks.com/weblinks** and select this book's title.

# Index